Reykjavik Tourism

Best Guide Iceland Trip

Carl Anderson

Copyright © 2017 by Kashvi Publishing, All rights reserved

All rights reserved. No part of this publication may be reproduced, distributed, or transmitted in any form or by any means, including photocopying, recording, or other electronic or mechanical methods, without the prior written permission of the publisher, except in the case of brief quotations embodied in critical reviews and certain other noncommercial uses permitted by copyright law. For permission, direct requests to the publisher, addressed "Attention: Permissions Coordinator," at the address below.Distribution of this book without the prior permission of the author is illegal, and therefore punishable by law. 1st Edition

Disclaimer

Legal Notice: - The author and publisher of this book and the accompanying materials have used their best efforts in preparing the material. The author and publisher make no representation or warranties with respect to the accuracy, applicability, fitness or completeness of the contents of this book. The information contained in this book is strictly for educational purposes. Therefore, if you wish to apply ideas contained in this book, you are taking full responsibility for your actions.

The author and publisher disclaim any warranties (express or implied), merchantability, or fitness for any particular purpose. The author and publisher shall in no event be held liable to any party for any direct, indirect, punitive, special, incidental or other consequential damages arising directly or indirectly from any use of this material, which is provided "as is", and without warranties.

As always, the advice of a competent legal, tax, accounting or other professional should be sought. The author and publisher do not warrant the performance, effectiveness or applicability of any sites listed or linked to in this book. All links are for information purposes only and are not warranted for content, accuracy or any other implied or explicit purpose.

Table of Contents

Introduction to Reykjavik 7

    Planning the Trip 10

    Staying at Reykjavik – Comfort vs. Price 14

    Hotels 14

    Hostels 18

    Non-Traditional Accommodation 19

CouchSurfing 25

    Travel Options When You Are in Iceland 27

    Car 27

    BUS 30

    Boat 31

Reykjavik 33

    Museums 33

    Zoo 36

The Hallgrimskirkja 37

    The Perlan and the Saga Museum 40

Whale Watching 42

The Golden Circle 44

Explore Iceland 49

The Northern Lights 53

The Ice Lagoon – the Jökulsárlón 55

The Blue Lagoon 56

Another Good Spa—the Myvatn 58

Maelifell 60

Glaciers 62

Ice Caves 63

Eastern Iceland 65

Little Iceland – the Snaefellsnes Peninsula 68

Where to Stay When Exploring the Ring Road 70

Botanical Gardens & Laugardalur Valley 73

Hike Mt Esja 75

Heidmörk Nature Reserve 77

Viðey 78

Seltjarnarnes 79

Here some restaurant tips in Reykjavik: 81

Iceland on a Budget 94

Introduction to Reykjavik

Many travel guides start with long and boring chapters about Reykjavik's and Iceland's history, but since we are going to explore the city and most of the countryside, I am only going to provide you with a few basic pieces of information here. Reykjavik is the northernmost capital city in the world and is the center of the Republic of Iceland. Our main target for this trip is Reykjavik, but since it's not a huge city like most capitals, we are going to also discover the country, the home of the natural beauty of Iceland. If you go to Iceland from a big city, you are going to find Reykjavik to resemble a large town rather than a capital: its population is circa 130,000, which is about 60 percent of the whole nation's population. I'm certain that those who live in cities of millions of souls will find it to be peaceful and a relaxing change of pace. There are six towns that are a part of Reykjavik. You may find that this city is smaller than what you are used to, but it's a vibrant living place where every generation can find fun.

I was thinking hard to find a stereotypical joke or at least something catchy about Icelanders, but I failed. What I've heard about Iceland is that its people have a traditional drinking session usually on Friday, when they go from pub to pub and drink until they can't stand—or until the morning comes. Another common thing I've encountered regarding Iceland is that it's quite pricey. This latest fact is important, as we are going to plan our trip to Reykjavik and to parts of Iceland on a tight budget, so we have to find the best solutions not to exceed our limits and exhaust our wallet.

Reykjavik itself is relatively small. You could even say it's the edge of the world, and to be honest, you would be very close to the truth. However, as different airlines have launched direct flights to Reykjavik from all around the world, it has become an exotic, must-visit destination for millions of travelers. The fact that it's the northernmost capital makes the city unique, and Iceland may be the only country that has a growing territory—the volcanic lava extends the island's size. The volcanic activity, the spectacular landscape, and the Northern Lights make Iceland one of the trendiest vacation spots.

In this book, we are going to explore the capital city and the countryside of Iceland, and I will provide insight on all affordable accommodations, itineraries, and natural and man-built wonders. When a person, a couple, or a group plans a trip to a foreign country, it's always imperative to learn a bit about the country and to learn where you can eat and rest for cheap. By the end of this guide, you will get an overall idea about Iceland, and if you need help, keep this book so you can access it whenever you wish.

Planning the Trip

Visiting Iceland won't be a cheap trip, however, it doesn't have to be as expensive as many travelers report. If you plan wisely and you are not afraid of trying new things, you could easily find a lot of places to stay and people to help you and take you to different places, and of course, you can eat without breaking your budget. The first thing you have to decide is how long you would like to stay and when you want to go. A vacation of 7 to 10 days in Iceland is quite enough time to explore the capital city and the countryside and to enjoy your time without the need to be hasty. If you go after the peak season (July and August), you can find more affordable accommodation prices, and a lot of late-season packages became available. Renting a car also becomes affordable. Companies tend to hype the prices during the main season, so with a budget in mind, you should avoid that months. Also, if you go during the fall, you have a better chance to go on an ice cave trip.

You will find out quite soon that the most expensive thing about visiting Reykjavik is the cost to travel from the States to Iceland. Depending on the starting airport, the flight can cost from $1000–$2000 per person. According to my research, the flight from New York to Reykjavik takes about six hours. I strongly advise against traveling first class, or anything higher than standard economy, because by doing so, you might just end up spending your entire budget on plane tickets. You might find a really cheap flight to Europe and go to Iceland from there, but I recommend a direct route, as it only takes six hours, and if you book a late-night flight, you can start exploring Reykjavik in the morning. Usually, the most affordable flights are from KLM,

Iceland Air, Air France, and Delta. You could book a flight with other airlines, but as the journey isn't too long, you could do well with the cheapest so you have more money left in your pocket. Below, you can see the prices of a roundtrip from New York JFK to Reykjavik Keflavik International:

	For one	For Two
KLM/Delta	$1008*	$2016
Iceland Air	$1490	$2980
Air France	$1008	$2016

*The price includes taxes, fees, and all related expenses, except for baggage fees if you have more. These were calculated on the airlines' official pages. They reflect a round trip, from August 18 to August 30, 2016.

You can find cheap tickets from www.priceline.com and www.studenuniversse.com

Another way to travel is by weekly ferries from Europe to Iceland, but that's long and more expensive.

Visiting Iceland will require a lot of preparation and foresight, as it's not some next-state trip you can do any time you feel like. Because it is such a popular vacation target, you have to book everything in advance. Fortunately, the Internet and social media changed the ways things work, so you can find a one-night bed for yourself at any time, and there are always eager locals who you can ask for directions and help. If you don't add the plane tickets' price to the recipe, it's possible to spend time in Reykjavik and spend about 55–65 dollars a day.

So now that you are ready to fly, it's time to see where you can stay. Iceland has been evolving, and it's one of the few countries that seem to be able to stand up from the devastation of 2008's crises. Nowadays, there are hundreds of Airbnb and CouchSurfing opportunities in

Reykjavik, while the countryside has farms and apartments for you to stay in. Together with food and drink, the accommodations are yet another cardinal part of your journey because they can affect the overall expenses of your visit.

Staying at Reykjavik – Comfort vs. Price

It's not easy to keep an Iceland vacation budget under control, but it is possible, and most importantly, you shouldn't let money stand in the way of exploring this cold, small paradise on earth. With social media ruling our lives, Internet access in our hands, and a wireless network at almost every corner, it just takes a few minutes to find a place to stay—not just in the States, but in Europe, and even in Iceland, too!

Hotels

I'm a traditional person, and when we started to look for a good place to stay, we started with hotels and apartments listed by the dozens on the Trip Advisor website. We planned our stay for nearly two weeks, from August 18to30, so the prices I mention here are reflective of that period. By the way, this 10-day period (the first and last days are mostly flying) is just enough to explore everything there is to see in Iceland. We usually rely on the crowd's opinion, so from the 59 hotels listed on Trip Advisor, we would choose from the first 10, as we don't believe that these sites are just about revenue, and the reviews are biased. For 10 days, or even a week-long stay, hotels in Reykjavik are not exactly what you might choose—at least we wouldn't actually stay in one because even the cheapest ones cost more than $100 per night for two, and there are substantial differences between them.

Generally, Hotel Smari is the cheapest hotel. This hotel received good and bad reviews alike, and it is only cc. $110–140 per night for two. Apart from being a two-star hotel with a bed and breakfast service included, one of its major benefits is that it's only a five-minute walk from the airport; however, being close to the airport also means it's quite far from downtown Reykjavik (five kilometers), so to dwell in the nightlife or explore the capital city itself, you either need to rent a car or hop on a bus (the bus stop is about 10–15 minutes away). As we looked for hotels closer to downtown, we found that the nightly prices were way too high for our budget, and we didn't want to spend more on the accommodation, the food, and the activities than we spent on the plane tickets. This means we had to keep our additional expenses under the $3,000 mark. Staying in hotels is a bit of a luxury many of us can't afford, but it's good to know what to expect if other solutions fail.

If you insist on staying in a hotel, and you would like to be as close to the city as possible, here is a list of options:

Hotel	Price Range* (for 2 people, per night)
Hotel Smari	$100–$140
Metropolitan Hotel	$130–$180
Icelandair Hotel Reykjavik Natura	$165–$180
Reykjavik Lights Hotel	$200–$220
Hotel Reykjavik Centrum	$195–$250
Storm Hotel	$225–$260
Eyja Guldsmeden Hotel	$225–$300

* The price range highly depends on the booking site you use. Check the cheapest one and see the chosen

hotel's site, too, because it might have a better package or discount.

Hostels

We were a bit surprised to find out how many hostels are available in Iceland. During the summer period, many schools and colleges turn their dormitories into hostels where you can spend a night for a friendlier price—if you don't mind making your own food and sharing the bathroom with others. The www.Hostel.is is the best place to find and book hostels throughout Iceland. Becoming a member is a must since you get some discounts.

Compared to hotels, the hostels of Reykjavik are somewhat expensive: during the summer, a double room costs 11500 Icelandic Krona (ISK), which is about 97–98 dollars per night—and that's the member price; the non-member prices start at 12000. This price doesn't include line nor breakfast, but you can book them for a hefty price. Important note: bring your own bed sheets or a sleeping bag with you because hardly any of the "traditional" accommodation options include them. The hostels' most welcomed benefit is that they are available throughout the country, and they cost the same throughout, so you can plan and calculate costs easily. Also, hostels are available near the center of Reykjavik, so you could explore the city from a place you could quickly return to. During the winter (after September 14), the prices of hostels are a bit lower, usually within 1000 ISK (cc. $8), and that makes this type of accommodation a fine choice for a few nights during the off-season. There are hostels all the way on the Iceland Ring Road, which follows the coastline, so if you plan to take a tour, hostels are always available.

Non-Traditional Accommodation

There are two newer ways to rest in Reykjavik (and throughout the world): Airbnb and CouchSurfing. Both are quite recently developed ways of renting, and among the two, Airbnb is the more traditional. Airbnb is a website where hosts can offer their "extra space," a bedroom, or apartment to travelers who can rent for a lower price than it would cost to stay in a hotel or hostel. Though Airbnb is a cheap and quite fine solution, it has one issue that probably won't concern you too much: its killing living in Reykjavik. Everyone who has an empty apartment, flat, or house rides the Airbnb horse and tries to profit from the fact that Reykjavik has become a very popular travel destination. And since everyone rents, there are hardly any buyable homes in Reykjavik. But as I said, this is something you don't have to worry about—it's not your fault that everyone tries to seize the opportunity. Below, the map shows some of the Airbnb opportunities of Reykjavik. The room prices are set per night, and it looks like a room where two guests could stay costs the same too, if not stated otherwise. If you open the Airbnb website, you can search yourself. Every place has a profile page where additional details are provided, and if you are going to travel with someone else, you should check the prices and the line "extra people."

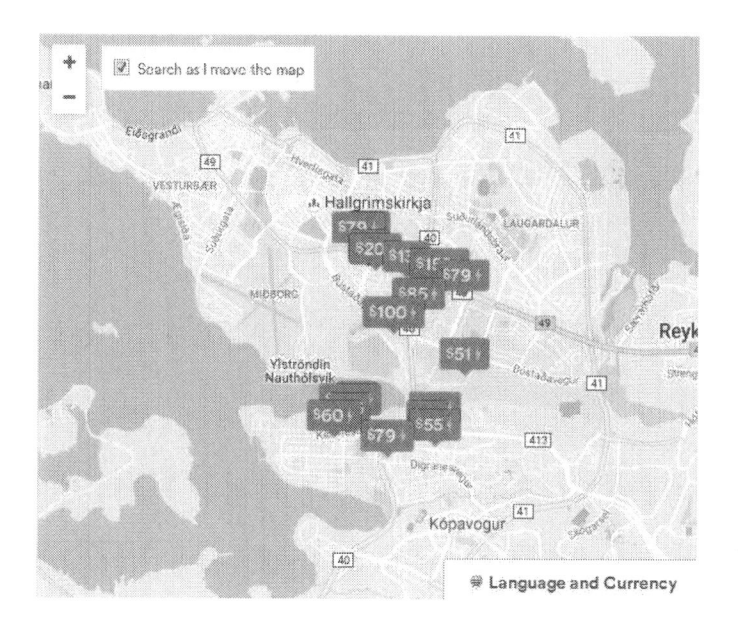

Airbnb, in fact, is much cheaper than hotels and hostels, and most of these locations are really near the center, the downtown, of Reykjavik—in most cases, a 10-minutes' walk and you are in the middle of the town or at the ocean! You can book your room on this website: https. This is a community, so in case you have any queries, you can ask, and fortunately, there are reviews so you know what you can expect. I was relieved when I first searched for Airbnb in Reykjavik because I found it to be an inexpensive solution, though booking in the main season is very, very hard. There are always new hosts appearing on the site, and since Airbnb is a regulated moneymaking opportunity, you can rest assured that you are doing it legally. You don't have to worry about being busted during a raid of the taxation office. ☺

There are a few side notes about Airbnb that you have to check before you book:

- ☐ There is always a requirement on how long you must stay, and though it's mostly one night, there are hosts who require two to three nights at minimum.

- There are house rules (you can see them on the site), which cover smoking, parties, and pets, and unfortunately, at most places, you can't do any of these. If you have your pet with you or if you smoke, be sure to check these rules. You may be able to find places to stay if you have a pet with you, though you will have your are freezing while you smoke outside.
- Apart from what you see on the search results page, additional fees may appear, such as for cleaning, bringing another person, and so on.
- You might have to share the bathroom with the hosts and their family.
- At most places, you can cook, which is important because cooking your own is more budget friendly, and breakfast is usually not included.

- There are three types of places: full apartments, private rooms, and shared rooms. The prices vary according to this and a few other factors.

CouchSurfing

This is the most inexpensive way to stay in Reykjavik or in the countryside, as it's usually free! CouchSurfing is a child of social media, and it's a kind of community event because there are groups of hosts who can offer you a couch or a bedroom to stay in. In exchange, you either invite your hosts to your own place later, or you may have to do some work around the house. There is an official website for surfers where you can see how many people are offering a chance to stay (about 5,000 in Iceland and Reykjavik), and you can also see what they offer. Registration is free, and it's necessary because you can only view hosts' full profiles if you have signed in. When you are looking for a place to stay, CouchSurfing is pretty much the best idea; however, if you plan to go with your beloved or a friend, you might want to check the host's availability and capability for hosting two.

CouchSurfing in Reykjavik has evolved into a really great thing, and there is a solid core that regularly comes together to host events like the weekly pub crawl or a road trip if there are any volunteers. The best feature about the CouchSurfing website is that you can share your ideas. And since Iceland is quite popular, you can get some folks to join you, so renting a car and staying won't cost you that much, as you share the expenses. If a host asks for money, you will be able to handle it, but as it's a community, a bad review can ruin their profile, so everyone stands true to the rules.

To stay in Reykjavik for a few days, I would rather choose a cheap place from Airbnb than try to couch surf through the countryside, staying and hanging out with locals. It's surely a much better experience and makes a traveler feel like home. In summary, these accommodations range from $100 per night to even free, which means that in the case that you are not an introvert, you can cut your expenses big time and have more to spend. Let's assume you have your accommodations booked; now it's time to find out how you can travel around Iceland.

Travel Options When You Are in Iceland

Car

There are many car rental options in Iceland, so if you are not a fan of mass transport, this is the optimal choice. There are several car rental companies, and as you will see, there are lots of sites where you can see all the prices and book your rental, so you don't have to worry about it later. Iceland has a good state road, and you can travel around freely without getting lost. The first thing you have to decide is where you are going to go in Iceland. If you stay in Reykjavik, you shouldn't even really need a car, but if you plan to explore elsewhere (e.g., the Golden Circle), it's advised to rent a car. There are 4x4 cars for $100–$150 per day, which you can take on trips with harder terrain, so exploring the countryside will be easier. You may rent city cars if you don't plan on going too far from the cities, thus you can enhance the quality of your stay.

One of the most popular car rental services is SadCars. I have seen mostly good reviews on this company, and it seems that they can even arrange accommodation for you, so if you are looking for packages with bed and car, you can find it with them. However, there are others who offer you comfortable cars and some extras for free. Apart from the car rental companies, you can rent cars from locals too, sometimes at a cheaper cost than from a company. At Cario.com, you can find a listing of Icelanders who are happy to rent their cars to you during the summer and winter. In off-season periods (from September to May), the rentals are cheaper from individuals and companies too.

Another way to get yourself a ride is carpooling or ride sharing. There are already a number of sites specialized for this field where you can find fellow travelers or locals who are looking to cut their expenses by sharing their car or renting a car together with others. As a last-minute resolution, you may look around at the CouchSurfing website, or attend an event, visit a hostel, and try to get some buddies to help you out. Icelanders are quite nice, and it's guaranteed that you can find a ride. For shared rides, check out travbuddy.com and samferda.net. The latest one is quite a simple page, while TravBuddy is a complex solution with community features, so you can prepare for what to expect from your ride.

Taxies are available too, but they are not recommended for longer travels, as they are quite pricey.

A single bus ride costs 420 ISK (~$3.5) in the capital, but you can also pay passes: there is a 20-ticket pass for about $68, but if you stay in Reykjavik, you could also buy one- or three-day passes for $13 or $30,

Which are valid for the chosen time period, and in the near vicinity of the capital? There is tour bus

Length	Price
24 hours	3,500 ISK (cc. $30)
48 hours	4,700 ISK (cc. $40)
72 hours	5,500 ISK (cc. $47)

BUS

Opportunities too, so in case that's your thing, the $60–$80 isn't too much for a comfortable ride around the city and the Golden Circle.

There is a special option for Reykjavik though, called the Reykjavik City Card. It's cheap, and it offers a lot of features, including unlimited bus passage throughout the capital. This card grants free entry into museums and some great discounts (we will get into details a bit later). See the table below for the prices:

Boat

Sailing is a very exciting experience, and I will try it as soon as I get the chance. Iceland is an island, so it has several ports. With this being said, you can rest assured that you can live out your sailing urges too. There are dozens of boat tours around Iceland that cover most of the things you should see when visiting the country. You can go on whale watching tours starting at $70 and daylong voyages around the island for $200. Also, there are Northern Lights–seeing tours starting from $95. I don't do this for any affiliate incomes or the likes, but Trip Advisor has a website dedicated to boats and sea trips. On Viator.com, you can find almost all available and bookable trips, and you might also receive discounts for booking there. When you visit Iceland, you shouldn't miss the whale watching and those weird yet cute puffins. For some extreme fun, you can even take kayaking tours in glaciers.

These are all the options you can consider for traveling around Iceland and in Reykjavik. There isn't a public railway system, so that's out of the roster. You have to stay on well-maintained roads. Now, let's see what you can do and see in Reykjavik; then we are going to explore the rest of the island in detail.

Reykjavik

As one of the smallest capitals of the world, Reykjavik is not so crowded, but it has everything a capital should have. There are museums, pubs, and many adventures waiting for you to explore. The culture of Iceland is interesting: its history is rich, and while you are in the capital, you will never experience a dull moment.

Museums

To explore the culture and legacy of Iceland, you should visit the museums throughout the city. With the Reykjavik City Card, you can enter many museums for free, so that's a pretty good deal for all culture seekers and learners.

- **The Reykjavik Art Museum**: You gain a free entry to the Hafnarhus, Kjarvalsstadir, and Asmundarsafn. The Hafnarhus is the home of the Kingdom exhibition, featuring old artistic drawings of the fauna of Iceland, and it also hosts Erró's work in the *Making of Erró* exhibition. (Erró was a popular pop-culture artist.) At the Kjarvalsstadir, you can browse the work of modern culture paintings and sculptures, including the work of the well-known artist, Johannes S. Kjarval. The Asmundarsafn is dedicated to Asmundur Sveinsson, and it's actually located in the former artist's home and studio.
- **National Museum of Iceland:** As most national museums, this one also features a

permanent exhibition about Icelandic history, called the *Making of a Nation – Heritage and History of Iceland*. Periodic exhibitions are usually featured too.

- **National Gallery of Iceland:** A place where you can get to know the culture of Iceland a bit more. You can explore the gallery's permanent exhibitions, and if you've never seen a Picasso in your life, you might just be in time to visit before it closes.

- **Reykjavik City Museum:** With the city card, you gain access to the Settlement Exhibition, the Árbaer Open Air Museum, the Museum of Photography, and the Maritime Museum.

During the time you stay at Reykjavik, you should visit a few of these exhibitions and get an insight on Icelandic culture.

Zoo

Reykjavik is the home of the Reykjavik Zoo and Family Park, and the Reykjavik City Card grants you a free entry to this. It's not huge, but it's worth a try, especially if you are traveling with children. The Family Park area has exciting activities like water bubbles, boats on water, and a few more. The zoo has a large collection of Icelandic animals along with some foreign reptiles.

The Hallgrimskirkja

The Hallgrimskirkja is a Lutheran church in Reykjavik, and it's the highest building in all of Iceland at 73 meters tall. The view is spectacular, and in case you are someone who loves a good sight, then you shouldn't miss it. It was finished in 1986, so it's not an ancient church, but its look resembles the flows of basalt lava that dot the landscape of Iceland. The admission fee to get up to the tower is cc. $4, and while you are there, you might also take a look at the famous pipe organ, which they used to play for tourists. If you ask a local, he or she can easily tell if the weather is prime for going up and enjoying the view, or if you should come back later. Beware of strong wind and blizzards, which can make the experience an extreme adventure.

For those who are interested in religious places and would like to implement some pilgrimage-like feeling into their journey in Reykjavik, there are a few other churches to explore: the Landakotskirkja is in Reykjavik's downtown, and it's one of the Catholic churches of Iceland. Though it's not an old one (finished in 1929) the hundred-year-old look makes it just as magical as those very old European churches and cathedrals. You might love the Fríkírkjan church near the Tjornin River, which is one of the oldest churches of Reykjavik, built in 1901. The oldest religious place to see in Reykjavik is the Domkirkjan

Cathedral, which has stood since 1796 and has a special historic value: this was the place where the national anthem was first sung, and Iceland's independence was first endorsed.

The Perlan and the Saga Museum

The Perlan is a tourist attraction and shopping center near downtown. The building is modern and spectacular. Inside, you can visit three shops, and you can rest your eyes on the wonderful scenery from the viewing deck (there are panoramic telescopes too). There is a winter garden in the building where they hold exhibitions and concerts.

In the Perlan, you can find the Saga Museum. It's a wax museum featuring characters related to Icelandic history. It's quite large, and apart from the sculptures, you can learn about Iceland's history with the audio guide. Those who like to shoot photos can even try on armor and authentic clothes!

REYKJAVIK TOURISM

Whale Watching

This is one of the most exciting experiences in Reykjavik. You can go on a whale watching tour from other parts of the country too, but since you are in the capital, why go anywhere else? You can book tickets online, but usually, you can buy them at the office on the day you have the time to go on the tour. In most cases, the agencies offer a second trip guarantee: you can go on another trip if you don't see any whales during your first. It's a very kind gesture and makes it worthwhile. Whale sighting usually goes on for about 3–4 hours, and if the crew spots a whale or a group of whales, the boat follows for 30–45 minutes. Also, during the trip, you might see puffins and sometimes dolphins too. The whale sighting tours are one of the main reasons why people visit Iceland, and nowadays, they are pretty affordable.

REYKJAVIK TOURISM

The Golden Circle

The Golden Circle of Iceland is a very popular tour. Many visitors take it by tour bus or by rented (or owned) cars. The basic circle is about 300 kilometers long, and it covers many "Icelandic" landscapes. It's a daylong tour, but if you want, you can spend a night somewhere so there is no rush, and you can enjoy the view and gather many experiences. There are thousands of guides for the Golden Circle online, and depending on the budget and time you have, you can visit different destinations and do many things to expand the basic route. Take your time and enjoy it: the biggest killer of fun is the rush. Driving on this route takes about three hours, and with stops, you will expand it to a full-day trip, which is totally worth it. The roads are not too busy—only getting out of the city might cause you a bit of a headache, but that's the only busy part of this journey. Basically, a full tank is enough for the ride, which is good news, as the fuel is quite expensive at $7 per gallon. You can download offline maps, and most car rentals have a GPS for you to rent for easier navigation.

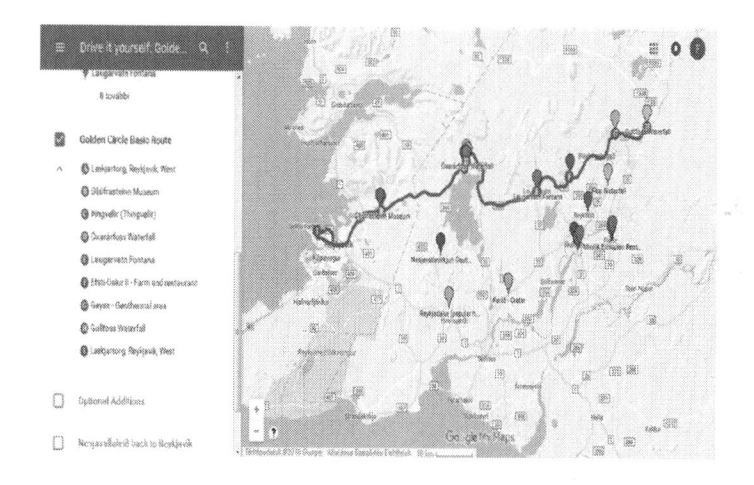

The first thing to do is to leave Reykjavik. The easiest way is to go north on Route 1 North until you reach the Miklabraut (route 49); then you have to head towards Þingvellir (a right-hand turn). At Þingvellir, you can see two things: a beautiful lake and a tectonic fissure called Almannagjá, where the Viking Parliament used to have its sessions. Just before you reach Þingvellir, you can see the estate of Halldor Laxness, Nobel Laureate of Iceland.

The road will get you to these wonderful destinations:

- **Kerid**: a volcanic crater filled with water. At least that's what people from Iceland believe. Recent studies proved that it probably was an actual volcano, which emptied its magma chamber and collapsed, thus creating the lake surrounded by spectacular red rocks.
- **Bruarfoss**: a wonderful waterfall. This is an area with strong geothermal activity, and there are agricultural and horticultural establishments throughout the land. The Bruarfoss waterfall can be reached only on foot, so if you visit in the winter, pack up some good boots and waterproof clothes.

- **Geysir**: this geothermal area holds many wonders, such as the Strokkur geyser and colorful hot springs. Also, if you go with a Jeep, you can go to the highlands, look around, and really feel like you are at the edge of the world.
- **Gullfoss Falls**: this waterfall is a preserved waterfall of Iceland. A hydropower plant was in plans to be built in here, but after a brave movement of a local girl, they decided not to. Now this two drop waterfall is one of the most spectacular things to see near Reykjavik.

There are several other stops you can make. If you plan to drive yourself, you can find lots of useful advice online and there is bus tours, which can give you an idea of where to start. This chapter was all about planning and moving around in Reykjavik, so it's high time to see the country itself and explore more of Iceland.

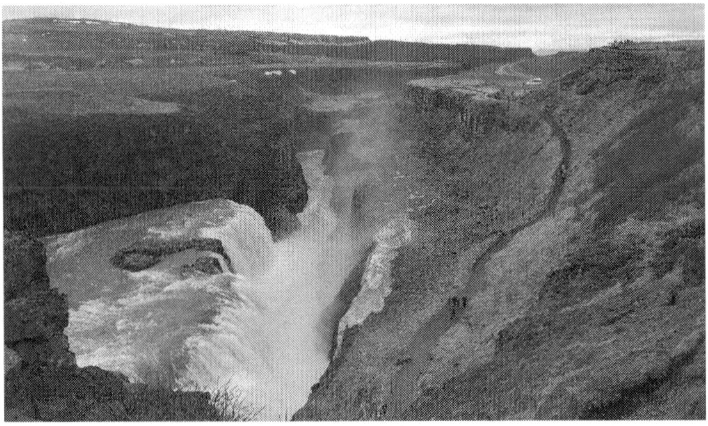

Explore Iceland

Iceland is not huge, and if you have limited time and a limited budget, you might have to resort to staying near Reykjavik and taking only a few guided tours. For longer periods, however (and with over $2000 spent on plane tickets), it would be the best to plan for a week at least. On the first two days, you can explore Reykjavik, the Golden Circle, and go whale sighting. Then, you'll want to make time to see the Northern Lights and all the other wonders this cold piece of paradise has in store for you.

Before we get on the road, we have to talk about something you can't live without: food and drink. Since Iceland doesn't have a strong agriculture due to its climate, it has a high import rate, which also means that food is somewhat expensive. As we are going on a budget, we have to watch our pockets, and after eating at a restaurant, you will come to the same conclusion as many others before: it's among the most expensive parts of an Iceland vacation. At most hotels, hostels, and apartments, you have access to a kitchen where you can prepare your food. Also, it might be a good idea to aim for accommodations that include breakfast and don't charge extra for it. You can buy ingredients at the local store chain's shops. The bonus—you can aim for food that has been produced inland, and they are much cheaper. Naturally, if you are looking for delicacies, you can try a few, but be careful, as you could eat away your money quickly. There are many hot dog stands in the cities, so for familiar street food, you don't have to go far.

Drinking is also cardinal, and I don't mean alcohol. You shouldn't buy water in bottles—the natural, cold water that comes from the tap is clean and delicious. Get yourself a strong bottle or a metal flask and refill it. Water is free everywhere. Alcohol is expensive, so if you are on a budget like we were, you won't participate in bar crawls unless they are matched with a happy hour.

Exploring the whole country will take about nine days. Especially if you like to shoot photos, you are going to stop and go about every 5–10 minutes because the landscape is just spectacular! Whenever you see a sign with the word *foss* on it, you will stop, because *foss*means waterfall and you may have seen a lot, but you haven't seen them all, and Iceland has many waterfalls for you. The best way to explore the whole island is to take the Ring Road, which hugs around the island. There are bus routes on the Ring Road, and sometimes you can grab a package with accommodations included, but the best way is to go with a rented vehicle. Nowadays, you can also rent a van from Happy Campers, which has a bed and appliances installed, so you can stop and sleep whenever you want.

Now, let's see what you can do on the Ring Road. There is no such thing as a wrong direction, because as you go on, you will eventually come back to the starting point.

The Northern Lights

The colorful and magical phenomenon, the Northern Lights, usually appear during the winter period, and you don't have to travel too far to see them. Naturally, you can see them only during the night, and if you are on the road, you can just stop the car, lay on the trunk, enjoy the view, and meditate on life's wonders, miseries, and what you are going to do with your life; and don't say you "wanna rock" because that's an old joke. On Iceland, you can see the Aurora Borealis, which is caused by electrically charged particles from our sun entering the Earth's atmosphere. Researchers found that there are peak periods of this phenomenon: the last peak was in 2013, and the next peak is expected eleven years later, in 2024. So if you can't see them now, return later, as there is a high chance that it's going to be much more spectacular. Naturally, you can see them now too; the peak is just the period when the activity is strongest. Aurora lights are usually the most visible around midnight.

The Ice Lagoon – the Jökulsárlón

The Jökulsárlón is located in the southeast part of the island. This is a special lagoon: it's an ice flow where you can see the ice flowing into the sea. Recently, it has become a lake, and a deep one at that, as the melting ice expanded the lagoon's territory. You can shoot some spectacular photos or relax and let your mind wander as you hear the ice breaking as the pieces hit each other and drop into the sea.

The Blue Lagoon

An expensive but totally worthwhile spais the Blue Lagoon of Iceland. It's on the Reykjanes Peninsula, about an hour's drive from Reykjavik. The Blue Lagoon is a man-made center for relaxation and bathing, and it uses the superheated water from a lava flow, which is vented to the Svartsengi geothermal power plant's turbines, and then it goes to the lagoon. It's clear and mineral-rich, which makes it a popular ailment for those who have skin problems. The Blue Lagoon is a full complex with a restaurant and accommodation, and it's so popular that you have to pre-book in advance to get in. Also, there is a research facility where they create skin care products and research for cures for different skin disorders using the minerals of the lake. This popular spa shows that even a small country can get world fame, and nothing shows this better than its appearances in movies like *Die another Day* and TV series like *Keeping Up with the Kardashians* and *Britain's Next Top Model*. The black rocks, the steam, and the clear blue water make up a perfect opportunity to fill your eyes and your camera's memory card.

Another Good Spa—the Myvatn

This nature bath is a less expensive and less crowded spa in Iceland. The name means something like *lake of midges*, which comes from the simple fact that there are lots of midges around the lake in the summer. You have to drive a lot to reach it, as the Myvatn geothermal area is about 500 miles from Reykjavik, but it's natural and cheap, and it's a perfect destination to relax while you can also enjoy the spectacular landscape. Spend at least half a day here to explore this active volcanic area, the wildlife, and the wonderful lake itself. Rest, recharge, and then go on with the rest of the Ring Road, as it's nearly in the middle of the tour. The bird population is also something you should explore; photograph as much of them as you can.

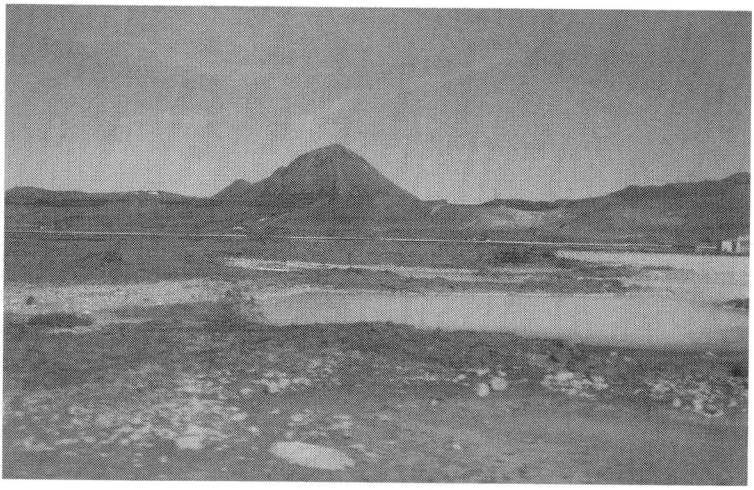

Maelifell

Have you ever seen a green volcano? If not, then you should time your visit to Iceland during the summer, because when the weather is warm, the snow melts away from this perfect cone-shaped volcano, revealing the mossy volcano side. The Maelifell is in the Myrdalsjökull Glacier Park, and apart from the main volcano, you can also watch and photograph other volcanoes and geysers. Since I'm talking about volcanoes, if you have room in your budget, you must book a ticket for a volcano flight. There are agencies that specialize in this, and if you are not afraid of flying above a real, active volcano, you can watch as Mother Earth shows her destructive yet creative power with lava eruptions. They look especially amazing in the dark, but the company won't fly you at night, so you have to watch them from a safe ground location or try to book the last flight of the day. They have flyovers for the recent Holuhraun eruption.

Glaciers

You will see glaciers during your trip throughout Iceland, and though they are great to look at, there is one thing you might like to try: glacier hiking. If you haven't done this before, you shouldn't try it alone, but fortunately, there are groups that offer you a chance—for quite reasonable prices—to climb a glacier. The experience is cold and wet, but the excitement will make up for all of the discomfort you may experience (like ice chips flying into your mouth as you climb).

Ice Caves

There are ice caves all across Iceland, but the most spectacular ones are the crystal ice caves. Do you recall Superman's Fortress of Solitude? Well, then you might know what to expect here. These caves are safe only during the winter, as the cold weather strengthens the ice. The most amazing caves are at the Vatnajokull Glacier, where you can opt-in for guided tours throughout the caverns with a patient guide, who will let you shoot those perfect photos of the clear blue ice caverns. You can go to ice cave exploring tours near Reykjavik too, so you don't necessarily have to leave the capital's area.

REYKJAVIK TOURISM

Eastern Iceland

The Eastern area of the island is a rugged place, and though there is a beaten track—according to other travelers—it feels like an off-track journey. The first stop for travelers is usually the city of Egilsstadir, as it has an airport and is kind of the center of this area. Outside the city, there is the lake called Lagarfljót, which is a great place to take photos of; and if you are lucky, you might even spot the Lagarfljótsormur, the giant worm that, according to legend, inhabits the lake since the times of the Vikings. However, he or she might have been extinct like poor Nessie of Loch Ness due to the climatic changes of the planet. On the eastern shore of Lagarfljót, you can take a trip or even camp in the biggest forest of the island, called Hallormsstadaskógur (yeah, these names are quite hard to write down and much harder to speak.). Though for an American the forest may seem small, it inhabits a significant part of this Island. As you travel through the East Fjords, you will find hypnotic landscapes. Pay extra attention to your surroundings, as wild reindeer roam the area. Interesting fact: though the reindeer look native here, the first ones were brought to Iceland from Norway about three centuries ago. Eastern Iceland is best traveled through with a local host, as he or she can tell you a lot of the myths and sagas about the area—stories of elves, ogres, and trolls, along with feuds and fled criminals of the icy shores.

The Blue Church of Seydisfjördur is quite famous, and if you travel there on Wednesdays in the summer, you can sit in and listen to some live music. The area is home to artists, and it's a fine place to buy some souvenirs.

Little Iceland – the Snaefellsnes Peninsula

Just before the road leads you back to Reykjavik, you have the chance to take a trip to the peninsula. There, you can find fishing towns, and one of the most photographed waterfalls in Iceland, the Kirkjufellsfoss. The Snaefellsnes Peninsula is also the home of the Snaefellsjökull National Park, where you can explore volcanic tubes, and if you long for a good hike, you can choose one from the many hiking trails. This peninsula is also the place where you can—according to Jules Verne—reach the center of Earth. In the novel, *Journey to the Center of the Earth*, Jules Verne named Snaefellsjökull, the highest icecap on the peninsula, to be the entrance to the center of the planet. You shouldn't try to go into the glacier, but if you arrive on a good day, you can take a guided tour.

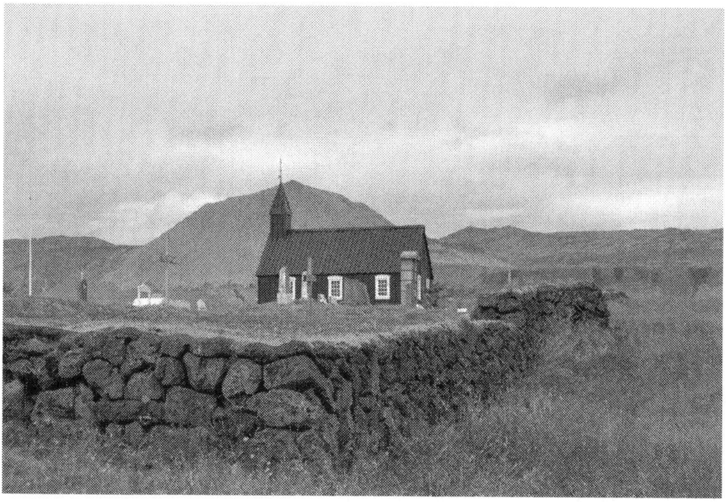

Where to Stay When Exploring the Ring Road

There are several towns on the coastline, and they are usually in safe driving distance from the road, so you can spend a night in hotels, hostels, or use an Airbnb or couch surfing option. If you go in the summer, you can also camp at several campsites. If you don't want to pay for the camping place, you could also wild camp. It's free, and you can set up your camp anywhere if it's not a protected natural reserve. When the weather is fine, you could try it for one night at least, but don't go camping in the winter or when it's raining.

Those who seek some work and also want to experience the wonders of Iceland could try to find a farmhouse. There are many farms and apartments that offer a room, food, and work to those who are looking for such things. The WWOOF (worldwide opportunities on organic farms) is a good place to find work and accommodations on Iceland; though there are only a few organic farms on Iceland, you have a chance to get to one. One of the most popular farms seems to be Eymundur Magnusson's farm in East Iceland. He usually has a place (and work) for sixteen, and he requires at least a three-week stay. You get accommodation, food, and of course, some free time, but there is also a lot of work to do. According to reviews and comments about this farm, it's one of the top destinations for WWOOFers. If you need experience, and you wish to gain insight to the future of agriculture, there is no better place than working at a farm in the harsh countryside of Iceland. (The picture doesn't feature this specific farm, but it's a farm on Iceland.)

REYKJAVIK TOURISM

Botanical Gardens & Laugardalur Valley

A beautiful oasis in Laugardalur Valley. The breadth of Icelandic flora on show, ponds and birdlife. Café on site during summer (May-September). Free entry. Located in the Laugardalur valley which is Reykjavík's main leisure area with numerous family-friendly attractions in one place such as Laugardalslaug thermal pool, Reykjavík Family Park & Zoo, Botanical Gardens, skating rink and football stadium. Extensive green areas, playgrounds and footpaths for walking, cycling and inline skating.

REYKJAVIK TOURISM

Hike Mt Esja

The 914-metre high mountain which presides over Reykjavík has stunning views of the capital area. This hike is very popular with Icelandic families. Don't forget to sign the guestbook at the peak! Note: Mt. Esja can be steep in places and there is occasionally some snow in summer. Follow routes closely and consider weather conditions before climbing. It is possible to reach Mt. Esja by by public transport: Take bus number 15 from Hlemmur bus station, get off at Haholt in Mosfellsbaer, then take bus number 27 to the foot of Esja at Esjumelar.

REYKJAVIK TOURISM

Heidmörk Nature Reserve

With its bushy vegetation, lava fields and caves, this extensive nature reserve on the outskirts of Reykjavík is popular for walks and family picnics. Playground, camping and barbecue facilities. Cross country skiing tracks in winter, snow permitting.

Viðey

Viðey is a small but impressive island with a long history, located in the nature reserve of Kollafjörður fjord inlet. It is just a 5-minute ferry trip from Reykjavík. Viðey's highest point rises 32m above sea level, and no fewer than 30 species of breeding birds have been spotted there. The island also provides a peaceful setting for leisurely walks and you will find a playground and picnic/BBQ area.

Seltjarnarnes

Seltjarnarnes is situated west of Reykjavík on the tip of the Reykjavík peninsula. Seltjarnarnes is, in addition to being a residential town, a beautiful nature reserve and recreation area where birds thrive in abundance: about 106 bird species stay in the area for shorter or longer periods. Seltjarnarnes is encircled by walking and cycling paths, with Grotta lighthouse and nature reserve located at one end, a small island that is accessible during low tide. There is a black stone beach that invites for a stroll and colecting shells and beautiful stones. Seltjarnarnes also offers a seaside golf course and thermal pool. From Seltjarnarnes one can enjoy amazing views over Reykjavik and its surroundings, and on a clear day it is possible to see all the way to Snaefellsnes glacier in the west - www.seltjarnarnes.is

REYKJAVIK TOURISM

Here some restaurant tips in Reykjavik:

Brassier Askur is a restaurant with fine dining and wine at moderate prices. Its location is at Suðurlandsbraut 4, near the Hilton Hotel Nordica, Grand Hotel Reykjavík and Park Inn Hotel Island, close to Hotel Cabin and Guesthouse Borgartún. This is a place where the locals go. Popular soup, bread and salad bar, lunch buffet Mondays through Fridays, Steak buffet every Sunday from 6:00 PM and menu every day full of variety. See: www.askur.is

Lækjarbrekka is a classic restaurant situated in the heart of Reykjavík in one of the oldest buildings in the city centre. The building has a remarkable history and there has been a restaurant here for twenty years. Lækjarbrekka restaurant creates the most delicious meals from the best possible Icelandic ingredients and provides first-rate service. There is a diverse menu from lunch time to evening, seven days a week. At lunch time they specialise in light, fresh dishes, such as soup or salad as well as fish and chicken dishes. In the afternoon the restaurant takes on a café atmosphere and a range of small dishes, sandwiches, coffee and cakes are available. In the evening, variety is the name of the game. Lækjarbrekka has everything from appetisers and vegetable dishes to sumptuous meat and fish dishes and there is something for all tastes. Old fashioned romantic atmosphere, outstanding modern Icelandic cuisine and excellent location in the heart of Reykjavík – this is a must go restaurant in Iceland's capital. See: www.laekjarbrekka.is

Dill Restaurant, a new Nordic restaurant located in the Nordic House in Reykjavík! DILL Restaurant is the mindful creation of Chef Gunnar Karl Gíslason and Sommelier Ólafur Örn Ólafsson, pioneers of the New

Nordic Kitchen in Iceland. Dill is much more than a restaurant. It is the result of a dream Gunnar Karl and Ólafur have shared for a while about a small restaurant with personality. A restaurant where guests not only eat well, but where the meal becomes an experience in itself and classic Nordic ingredients are prepared in a modern way with contemporary kitchen gadgets. We look forward to sharing our dream with you. Located near to Radisson Hotel Saga and Reykjavik Natura Hotel. See: www.dillrestaurant.is

Fiskfélagið – Fish Company: Adventure under a bridge, located in the city center next door to Hotel Plaza. In the early days of the Fish Company, a satisfied patron set his plate to the side and remarked; "Without fail, all the best adventures take place under a bridge." They immediately secured his permission to use this as their slogan. Not only is the menu an adventurous journey around the world, a sense of adventure is also reflected in the surroundings and essence of the venue. The Zimsen building dates back to 1884 and originally stood at Hafnarstræti 21, a few hundred meters east of its current location. It was extended in 1889, but in 2006 it was uprooted and lovingly renovated before being replanted at Grófartorg in 2008. During the groundwork stages of the Grófartorg reconstruction area, excavation unearthed remnants of the older harbour, which has now been incorporated into "The Tides", a work of art by Hjörleifur Stefánsson, developed in collaboration with Minjavernd Heritage Trust. This gives the area a unique atmosphere which is further emphasized as the tides come in and go out in the artwork as they do in the current harbour. The restaurant was designed by Leif Welding and master chef Lárus Gunnar Jónasson. Chefs are drawn to experimentation with contrasts and with Leif's expertise they created an exciting yet functional venue.

Window panes from the Hafnarfjörður Free Lutheran Church are backlit behind the bar, lending an adventurous light to their surroundings. The booths in the inner hall are made by GH húsgögn but the chairs are from Tom Dixon. Dinner is served on china from Figgijo in Norway, originally designed exclusively for the Fish Company, but due to their popularity they are now being manufactured for world wide marketing. Many of the items used in the restaurant, china and kitchenware alike, are on display and for sale in the outer hall. We are delighted to lead you through a world of culinary adventures, which, as most good adventures do, begins under a bridge. See: www.fiskfelagid.is

Þrír Frakkar, the restaurant Þrír Frakkar at Baldursgata 14 was opened on March 1, 1989 and has been run by the chef Mr. Úlfar Eysteinsson CF master Chef and his family since then. The restaurant is one of few restaurants in Iceland which has had the same owner for such a long time. The restaurant is conveniently located in the downtown area and is within walking distance of the major shops and services in the city center. The restaurant is located in the vicinity of most of the foreign embassies in Reykjavik, Hotel Holt and Hallgrímskirkja-church. The chef, Úlfar Eysteinsson, has always placed major emphasis on fish courses and the restaurant has become well known for its delicious fish fare. Other specialties on the menu include whale meat and sea bird entrees. The restaurant seats 44 guests and prides itself on its fine service. Prices are in the moderate range and the restaurant offers an inexpensive lunch menu. The restaurant is open Monday through Friday from 11:30 noon to 2:30 pm and 6:00 to 10:00 pm. On Saturdays and Sundays the restaurant is open between 6:00 pm. and 11:00 pm. See: www.3frakkar.com

Café Loki, located at Lokastígur 28 across from Hallgrímskirkja Church, is the complete Icelandic café with a menu which consists of Icelandic dishes. Café LOKI, opened in 2008, is a new and needed addition to Reykjavik's restaurant scene, just a 5 minutes walk from city center. Foreign guests visiting Reykjavík frequently look for restaurants to sample traditional Icelandic cuisine, not with much success. Search no more! Café LOKI does all that and more. At Café LOKI you find something affordable, tasty and completely Icelandic. The proprietor Hrönn Vilhelmsdóttir and her husband, Þórólfur Antonsson have found the right recipe to attract and impress both foreigners and Icelanders by using only Icelandic raw material. Þórólfur runs the coffee house with his wife and the homemade bread is his masterpiece. At Café LOKI You can choose from homemade food and bread, baked at LOKI, such as rye bread, flatbread and spelt bagels.

LOKI uses family 5 recipes, some more than 150 years old while others are new but with an old stylish touch. LOKI is both an ordinary café and an Icelandic specialty. You can enjoy herring, smoked trout, sheep-head jelly, Icelandic Plates I or II covered with all sorts of Icelandic staples. With a neat, airy décor and a splendid view of Hallgrímskirkja, Café LOKI is the perfect place to take a load off your feet and enjoy solid homemade Icelandic food. In the basement of Café Loki is a small handicraft & textile store with amazing and unique products made in Iceland. See: www.textil.is

Lauga-ás Restaurant, that's where the locals go. Restaurant Lauga-ás was established June 25th 1979 and is one of Iceland's oldest restaurants with the same owner from the start, Ragnar Kr. Guðmundsson. Lauga-ás is known for its fish items, variety in cooking and most of all, known for serving fish not available elsewhere. They serve hearty portions of fresh seafood.

Popular is also the lamb dish with béarnaise sauce. This restaurant is located near Hilton Hotel Nordica, Grand Hotel Reykjavik, Hotel Cabin, Guesthouse Borgartún, the Youth Hostel, very close to Laugardalur swimming pool. See: www.laugaas.is

Hamborgara Fabrikkan – Fancy the best hamburgers in Iceland? The Icelandic Hamburger Factory is a new restaurant overlooking the place where Ronald Reagan and Mikhail Gorbachev almost ended the Cold War. But that's history. Try the unique Hamburgers and the first Icelandic Lamburger. Great prices on food, beer and wine. Come and feel the Factory buzz. It's worth it. This place offers a kind of Hard Rock Café atmosphere – just very Icelandic; playing mainly Icelandic pop music. Located in the glass tower called Turninn at Höfðatorg on Borgartún Street, near to Fosshotel Lind, Fosshotel Baron, Best

Western Hotel Reykjavík, Guesthouse Borgartún, Grand Hotel and Hotel Cabin. See: www.fabrikkan.is

Argentína – Classy steakhouse with coal-grilled lamb, beef and fish courses. Cognac room. Located at Barónsstígur 11a, a side-street of Laugavegur shopping street, near to Fosshotel Baron, Fosshotel Lind, Best Western Hotel Reykjavík and Hotel Fron. See: www.argentina.is

Fish Market – Icelandic food prepared with a modern twist, using ingredients sourced directly from the nation's best farms, lakes and sea to create unforgettable Icelandic dishes. Housed in one of the city's oldest buildings and located in the city center at Aðalstraeti 12, between the Hotel Reykjavík Centrum and Hotel Plaza. See: www.fishmarket.is

Grillhúsið – A popular place by the locals. Ideal if you want to have an authentic American rock'n roll lunch or dinner at a good price. Located in the city center at

Tryggvagata 20, near to Hotel Plaza, Hotel Borg, Hotel Reykjavík Centrum and Radisson 1919. See: www.grillhusid.is

Lobster House / Humarhúsið – In the city center, just a few steps from Laugarvegur shopping street. A cosy restaurant in an old building which specialises in seafood and lobster. See: www.humarhusid.is

The Pearl – Fine dining in a revolving restaurant. Splendid view over the city. See: www.perlan.is

Seafood Grill, offers grilled fish, meat and vegetables from an award winning chef. Located in the city center at Skólavörðustígur 14 between Laugavegur shopping street and Hallgrímskirkja church. See: www.sjavargrillid.is

Vox – Gourmet dining at the Hilton Hotel Nordica. Award winning chefs. Mediterranean lunch buffet and sushi. Walking distance from Grand Hotel, Guesthouse Borgartún and Hotel Cabin. See: www.vox.is

Einar Ben, is one of Reykjavik's most elegant restaurants, located in one of the oldest trading buildings in the Icelandic capital. Einar Ben is named after one of the most remarkable Icelanders of recent times and we try to honour him by serving delicious food made from quality Icelandic ingredients: fish, seabirds, wild game and lamb. Service is relaxed but professional. Located in the city center near to Hotel Plaza, Hotel Reykjavík Centrum, Hotel Borg and Radisson 1919. See: www.einarben.is

Bæjarins Beztu – Close to the harbour and next door to Radisson Hotel 1919. It's the most popular hot dog stand in Reykjavík. You'll recognize it by the queue. This humble stand satisfies hunger to visitors and locals alike. We recommend getting one with everything - remoulade, mustard, fried onions and pickles!

Good to know

1. You can ask for a children's menu when dining out with little ones.
2. Tipping is not customary in Iceland since service is included in the price.
3. All restaurants, cafés and bars in Iceland are non smoking.
4. It is better to reserve a table in advance for the weekends.

Other good restaurant website:

www.restaurants.is

www.diningouticeland.com

www.dining.is

At the tourist information office and at most hotels you can ask for the DINING OUT brochure, a large booklet about restaurants & cafés around Iceland.

Iceland on a Budget

It's possible to explore those wonderful landscapes, natural events, and man-built items that Iceland can offer, even if you are on a budget. Most of the above-listed things are accessible for free, and if you plan to visit Iceland to be away from civilization, you just have to spend on food, accommodation, and transport. However, if you are comfortable with sharing your car with strangers, and you don't mind sleeping on others' couches, you can cut the expenses significantly. Truth to be told, I was thinking about the campervan renting—in the main season, it costs about $205 per day, and in mid- and off-season, the price is lower. The only problem is the fuel, but if you rent a normal car, you would need to refuel a few times as you travel around the island. A campervan might be the best choice for many reasons: you don't have to pay for accommodation, and you can cook your own food. Also, different from bus tours or car sharing, you can stop and go whenever you like, and you can just get to a parking place and sleep through the nastier blizzards.

One of the most important questions is whether Iceland is too expensive or not. It's one of the hardest questions, and there are many answers to it. Some would say without hesitation that it's a kind of trip only millionaires can afford, and basically, with today's economy, scraping together even the plane tickets' price could prove to be hard for those who work in low-paying industries (cc. $22,000 per year), but it's not impossible. Couples and families with both adults working could have a better chance to actually make it to Iceland, and they won't regret it.

Reykjavik with a Golden Circle tour alone is a great destination, but if you can afford it, and you have the time, you should visit other places on the island. If you want, you can take a plane from one end to the other (about an hour's flight) and then rent a car for the day and go as far as you can. Iceland is a land of wonders, and its isolated nature makes it the best destination for those who seek something different from the more hyped destinations.

Made in the USA
Lexington, KY
15 September 2017